People Who Have Helped the World

PETER BENENSON

by David Winner

For a free color catalog describing Gareth Stevens' list of high-quality children's books, call 1-800-341-3569 (USA) or 1-800-461-9120 (Canada).

Picture Credits

Amnesty International — 18, 19, 21 (both), 23, 24, 25, 30, 31, 32, 40 (Ted Jackson), 43, 45; AI Amsterdam — 54, 60; AI Japan — 26, 55; AI Secretariat — 4, 12, 16-17; AI Stockholm — 50; Andes Press Agency — 56-57, 57 (Carlos Reyes); Peter Benenson — 6, 7, 10, 27, 36, 53; The Bridgeman Art Library — 32; Canapress, Canada — 59; Jean Domique — 29; *La Presse Quebec* — 58; Magnum — 37 (Alex Webb): 48-49 (Stuart Franklin); The Mansell Collection — 35; Network — 33 (Goldwater); *The Observer* — 20; Popperfoto — 8 (both), 9, 15; Rex Features — 41 (lower, Ben Weaver); 49 (Fallander); Frank Spooner — 28 (E. Bouvet): 41 (top left and right): 52 (both, Ajanksi).

North American edition first published in 1991 by
Gareth Stevens, Inc.
1555 North RiverCenter Drive, Suite 201
Milwaukee, Wisconsin 53212, USA

Library of Congress Cataloging-in-Publication Data

Winner, David, 1956-
    Peter Benenson / by David Winner.
        p. cm. — (People who have helped the world)
    Includes index.
    Summary: Biography of the English-Jewish lawyer who founded Amnesty International, the organization dedicated to investigating and publicizing civil rights abuses the world over.
    ISBN 0-8368-0400-7
    1. Benenson, Peter, 1921- —Juvenile literature. 2. Civil rights workers—Great Britain—Biography—Juvenile literature. 3. Human rights workers—Great Britain—Biography—Juvenile literature. 4. Lawyers—Great Britain—Biography—Juvenile literature. 5. Amnesty International—History—Juvenile literature. [1. Benenson, Peter, 1921- . 2. Civil rights workers. 3. Human rights workers. 4. Lawyers. 5. Amnesty International—History.] I. Title. II. Series.
JC571.W477   1991
323'.092—dc20
[B]   90-47877

Series conceived and edited by Helen Exley
Picture research: Elizabeth Loving
Editors: Samantha Armstrong and Margaret Montgomery
Series editor, U.S.: Amy Bauman
Editor, U.S.: Patricia Lantier-Sampon
Editorial assistants, U.S.: Scott Enk, Diane Laska, John D. Rateliff, Jennifer Thelen

Printed in Hungary

1 2 3 4 5 6 7 8 9 95 94 93 92 91

PETER BENENSON

Taking a stand against injustice —
Amnesty International

by David Winner

Gareth Stevens Publishing
MILWAUKEE

A toast to liberty

Peter Benenson was sitting on a crowded London underground train when the article first caught his eye. It was a small item in the foreign news section of that day's *Daily Telegraph*. Then, as now, there were always several outlandish stories to read in most of the world's newspapers. But somehow this one made him sit bolt upright.

Two young students in a café in Lisbon had been extremely reckless. The wine they were drinking must surely have gone to their heads. In a public place where anyone might see them, the young men had stood up together and raised their glasses in a toast to liberty.

Any democratic country would consider such an act innocent and harmless. But Portugal at that time was not democratic. Its ruler, dictator Antonio Salazar, forbade all forms of political expression that he did not approve. And he most certainly did not approve of toasts to liberty. The two students had been instantly arrested, brought to court, and sentenced to seven years in prison.

Benenson was outraged. This was clearly an example of tyranny. He got off the train several stops early at Trafalgar Square, righteous anger boiling up inside him. His first impulse was to march directly to the Portuguese embassy to protest. But what good would that do? At best, some minor official would listen to his complaint and take notes. As soon as Benenson had left the building, his protest would probably be tossed out. He stopped for a moment. He had to think. He turned around and headed for the famous church in the corner of Trafalgar Square, Saint Martin-in-the-Fields, to decide what to do next.

Peter Benenson was a devout Christian, and he slowly calmed down as he faced the austerely beautiful altar. He was still shocked by the fate of the students,

"On 10 December 1948 the United Nations General Assembly proclaimed the Universal Declaration of Human Rights without dissent. The governments of the world agreed, for the first time in history, to a statement of every person's basic human rights. . . . They promised to work towards a world without cruelty and injustice.

"They didn't keep the promise. . . . more than half of the world's governments [jail] people in violation of their human rights. A third of the world's governments torture their prisoners."

John G. Healey, executive director of Amnesty International U.S.A.

Opposite: Amnesty International, created by Peter Benenson, stands for human rights all over the world. This powerful image of a man bound and jailed is from an Amnesty group in Nigeria.

5

but he started to concentrate on other thoughts and feelings about injustice that had been bubbling inside him for years.

By the time he left the church and walked slowly to his office, Benenson had thought of a plan. He had formulated an ambitious response to this Portuguese tyrant — and to tyrants everywhere. What Peter Benenson planned that day in November 1960 would grow into the biggest human rights movement in the world — Amnesty International.

The Benensons

Above: Peter Benenson as a child. Below: Flora Benenson had a charismatic personality and campaigned successfully for many good causes. After her husband's death, when Peter was just nine, she brought him up alone.

To anyone who knew him, Benenson's response to the newspaper article should have been no surprise. Not only was he a lawyer; he was also an idealist. He had earned a reputation as someone who went out of his way to help people who were being treated unfairly.

Peter Benenson came from a remarkable Russian-Jewish-English background. His grandfather, Grigori Benenson, had been a successful and respected multimillionaire banker and oil tycoon in tsarist times. This was a phenomenal achievement for a Jew in such a notoriously anti-Semitic country as Russia. It was in honor of this grandfather that Peter later decided to adopt Benenson as his legal surname.

Peter's mother, Flora, was another remarkable character. Her friends and acquaintances included charismatic, powerful, and idealistic figures of the day. She was a friend of Eleanor Roosevelt, the great champion of human rights and wife of U.S. president Franklin D. Roosevelt. She was close to the former Russian prime minister Alexander Kerensky and the first president of Israel, Chaim Weizmann. Flora was also an effective campaigner and had a great reputation for her unselfish work with charitable causes.

The Benensons had left Russia after the 1917 Bolshevik Revolution, when communism replaced the fledgling Russian democracy. Soon after World War I, Flora met Harold Solomon, a dashing British army officer. Solomon was an army colonel who later served as a government official. They were married after a whirlwind romance.

Peter was born in London on July 31, 1921. He was a happy, thoughtful child. When he was still a baby, his father suffered a terrible injury in a riding accident and was thereafter confined to a wheelchair. A few years later, Harold Solomon fell ill and died while on a trip to Switzerland. Peter, nine years old, was devastated.

After Harold's death, Flora became the main influence in Peter's life. Some of her dynamism, warmth, and idealism rubbed off on him. She made sure that he got a strong education. Before going to school, a famous poet — the young W. H. Auden — served as his private tutor. Later, Peter won a scholarship to Eton, the most famous of England's private schools, and then went on to study history at Oxford University.

Peter's quick mind and high intelligence were always appreciated. But his insistence that people should be treated fairly and his refusal to be intimidated by figures of authority caused some problems. At school, Peter was brave enough to complain to the headmaster about the poor quality of the school's food. The headmaster was surprised and wrote to Peter's mother, warning her about her son's "revolutionary tendencies." But Flora saw the incident as a sign of Peter's awakening social conscience, and she proudly encouraged him. Later, one of Peter's teachers predicted that his star pupil would one day write an "interesting and most vividly written" history book, but that it would probably cause much debate among scholars.

Peter Benenson as a young man. His school head-master saw "revolutionary tendencies" in Peter's demand for decent school food. By the time he was sixteen, Peter had launched his first campaign — to help victims of fascism in Spain.

The schoolboy campaigner

When Peter was sixteen, he launched his first socio-political campaign. The Spanish Civil War had started a year earlier. The democratic Republican government was fighting to stop a fascist rebellion led by General Francisco Franco, who would later rule the country as a dictator for nearly forty years. The Republicans were outgunned, and civilians on their side suffered terribly.

The struggle, which lasted from 1936 to 1939, was Europe's first taste of the kind of cruel, total war that would soon engulf the whole continent.

Peter was shocked by the brutality and illegal tactics of Franco's rebellion. Together with friends, he organized school support for the newly formed Spanish Relief Committee, which helped Republican children orphaned by the war. Peter's very first political act was to "adopt" a baby by agreeing to pay for his care.

By 1938, the menace of Nazi Germany was obvious. At school, Peter raised £4000 ($20,000) to save two German Jewish boys by bringing them to England. British immigration policies allowed some Jewish children to escape to freedom (right), but when the war came, millions of European Jews, including one-and-a-half million children, were rounded up and sent to death camps in Poland to be gassed (left).

Peter also read everything he could find about the war and soon passionately identified with the Republican cause. One book that particularly influenced him was Arthur Koestler's *Spanish Testament*, which described the horrors of imprisonment and execution by the Fascists. Peter was deeply depressed when the Republicans finally lost the war. At that time, the baby he had "adopted" was also lost.

Refugees

Soon, though, Peter had another mission — to help rescue some of the Jews who were trying to flee the anti-Semitic terror of Adolf Hitler's Nazi Germany. Even though German Jews were in terrible danger of losing their lives, Britain, like most other countries, locked its doors to all but a few of those who were trying to escape. Only refugees who were lucky enough to find British supporters willing to guarantee that they would not be a financial burden on the country were being allowed in.

Peter's new campaign was more ambitious than the last. His schoolmates and their families succeeded in raising about £4,000 ($20,000) — a huge amount of money in 1938 — to bring two young German Jews to school in Britain. There was surprising resistance from two quarters: from parents of Jewish boys at the school who feared that the campaign might in some way draw attention to the fact that they were Jews, and from the headmaster, who praised Peter's efforts but insisted that Eton couldn't take refugees from all over the world. Nevertheless, the Jewish boys were rescued and arrived in Britain. One later became an electrical engineer and one of Peter's lifelong friends. The other now lives in Australia, where he works as a chef.

Military service

Most other European Jews were less fortunate. As the plight of the Jews became increasingly urgent, Britain agreed to let in ten thousand Jewish children. Peter left Eton as soon as he was able and went to work helping some of the new child refugees arriving in London. His job was to find new homes for them in other parts of the world, so that more children would be allowed into Britain. Every one of them who could escape from Nazi-occupied Europe was a life saved. But most of the families they left behind were soon to be murdered, along with a total of six million other Jews.

At the beginning of September 1939, Adolf Hitler's Nazi forces invaded Poland. As soon as war was declared, Peter volunteered for the Royal Navy. To his amazement, he was initially refused because his mother had been born in Russia. Instead, he enrolled in classes at Oxford University.

Peter Benenson was accepted for military service in 1940 in spite of his Russian ancestry. His first job was in the Ministry of Information press office and then, when the Soviet Union joined the war effort, at the top secret intelligence unit that deciphered secret German communication codes. Benenson's unit played a crucial part in the war against Nazism. His job at the ministry had a personal significance, too. He and his future wife Margaret met there.

The war finally ended in 1945. But because of a rule that allowed older men to leave the army first, twenty-four-year-old Benenson could not go back into civilian life immediately. He studied law to keep himself from

Nazi dictator Adolf Hitler preached racial hatred and wanted to conquer the world. In 1939, when he ordered the invasion of Poland, Britain and France declared war on Germany. World War II continued until 1945, and during those six years an estimated fifty-five million people lost their lives.

Peter Benenson as a British soldier in 1941. He was turned down when he volunteered for the Royal Navy, but later joined a military intelligence unit and helped to crack top secret Nazi communication codes.

getting bored. By the time he left two years later, he was ready for a career as a lawyer. He also followed his mother's example and became passionately interested in politics and joined Britain's Labour party. His law training and imaginative socialist ideals now began to take him into new areas.

Peter Benenson, lawyer

Franco was trying to destroy Spain's small underground trade union movement. Members of the British Trade Union Congress (TUC), eager to help their embattled colleagues, asked Benenson to act as their official observer at a trial of trade unionists in Spain. The trial was a mockery of justice and Benenson's presence made little difference as to the result — the trade unionists were sent to prison. But Benenson did well enough for the TUC to send him back later to observe similar trials in Spain.

As an observer, Peter Benenson's power to influence events for the better was limited. But he soon learned to make his presence felt. He helped the defendants by insisting on his right to see crucial documents and making it clear that he disapproved of unfairness. He also witnessed the dreadful conditions in Spanish prisons and made himself a friend to prisoners' families. On his return to Britain, Benenson persuaded the TUC to set up a special committee to help these new victims of the Franco regime. He found several members of Parliament who were eager to help. Benenson himself became the group's secretary.

His next visit to Spain was for the trial of a very different set of prisoners. Once again, all the odds were against the defendants. At first, Benenson was denied entrance to the courtroom. But he demanded to be let in and was allowed to stand at the back. He was shocked by what he saw. That night he drew up a list of complaints, went straight to the judge's hotel, and confronted him as he was eating his dinner. The astonished judge almost choked on his soup as Benenson told him exactly what he thought of the unfair way the trial was being handled. The judge took his seat the next morning looking like a ghost, and the trial ended with the defendants being set free — almost unheard of in a political trial in Spain at the time.

Justice

Peter Benenson's reputation continued to grow, and he became busier than ever. Many foreign clients solicited his services. He gave advice and help to Greek lawyers from the island of Cyprus whose clients had disobeyed British rule. His interest in civil liberties was growing and, as a leading member of the Society of Labour Lawyers, he found sympathetic colleagues. The other main British political parties, the Conservatives and Liberals, also had similar groups.

In 1956, Benenson persuaded the three parties to put aside their differences and work together. News came from South Africa that 156 opponents of the racist system of apartheid, including Nelson Mandela, had been accused of treason and were about to go on trial for their lives. Meanwhile, an uprising in Hungary had been suppressed by a bloody Soviet invasion.

The two crises attracted different political sympathies. Left-wingers were outraged about South Africa. Conservatives were up in arms about Hungary, where the bloody invasion was soon followed by a wave of political trials and executions.

Peter Benenson saw that both situations demanded action. So he persuaded the Liberal, Labour, and Conservative lawyers to work together to send observers to both countries. Benenson went to Hungary while a more senior lawyer, Gerald Gardiner, went to South Africa. The move was such a success that Benenson was able to form a new, independent group to carry on similar work wherever necessary. It was called "Justice." Justice later became the British section of the International Commission of Jurists.

Birth of a notion

Benenson's work for victims of unfair trials and other types of injustice had made him realize that action was needed on a much larger scale.

In 1959, shortly before his thirty-eighth birthday, Benenson fell seriously ill with a rare throat and stomach disease called tropical sprue. His doctor ordered him to take six months off to recuperate, and he went to Italy. He used the move to give up his legal career. He joked: "In six months my clients will have found other and probably better barristers." In fact, the

"Anyone who has worked in a newspaper or a government knows that getting the 'facts' is extraordinarily difficult. Yet the number of times Amnesty has been shown to be badly misinformed are few and far between. Western diplomats growl under their breath about Amnesty exaggerations, but the criticism never seems properly to surface."

Jonathan Power, in his book
Amnesty International: The
Human Rights Story

law had never been his major interest, and he would now be free to concentrate on activities that interested him more directly.

New ideas began to take root as Benenson relaxed in Italy. Serious lawyers' organizations were very helpful, he reasoned, but they were too slow and cautious ever to fire the public imagination. There must be a more dramatic and effective way to help people and to get thousands of ordinary, concerned citizens involved.

The newspaper story about the Portuguese students appeared in November 1960, a month after Peter's return to London. It affected him very deeply. All his ideas rushed into focus as he sat alone in the church of Saint Martin-in-the-Fields. Benenson remembered how an international campaign called World Refugee Year had helped to find homes for the last of the millions of refugees from World War II. Why not help the Lisbon students and all the other victims of such oppression by launching another worldwide campaign — this time for the release of political prisoners? The most powerful weapon Benenson planned to use was publicity. His campaign would employ a barrage of public opinion and front-page news articles to apply pressure to tyrannical governments.

This campaign — Amnesty International — now the most respected and effective human rights movement in the world, was about to be born.

An appeal to the world

Benenson excitedly discussed his plan with friends. Some dismissed the idea, but others immediately offered to help. Someone suggested that they call the campaign "Appeal for Amnesty, 1961."

Benenson and his colleagues began to make plans for a short, powerful one-year campaign to orchestrate the release of political prisoners all over the world. The formal launching of this campaign was set for May 28, 1961, only a few months away. Benenson's network of friends helped him recruit some of the brightest and most idealistic people in Britain. There were lawyers like Louis Blom-Cooper, and Peter Archer, a future member of Parliament. Others had no legal background, like the legendary British journalist, James Cameron,

"It seems to be in the nature of oppression that the very individuals who would effect positive change for the future are the people Amnesty has to protect."

Sting, musician and conservationist

Opposite: After World War II, Peter Benenson became a lawyer. His offices at 1 Mitre Court in London became the focal point of lawyers' human rights work and were Amnesty International's first headquarters.

13

and an influential Quaker activist, Eric Baker, who became one of Benenson's main partners.

Peter Benenson was a private and modest man and in later years would avoid personal praise and publicity. But he had incredible energy, charisma, and a gift for pulling people together. The new group's members met regularly for lunch to talk about their goals. With Benenson in charge, they bubbled with ideas and enthusiasm. Great moral and practical decisions for the coming campaign had to be made. Who would they fight for? And how? Someone scribbled notes on a paper napkin as the conversation blazed.

Peter Benenson's charm, energy, and astonishing capacity for ideas sparked the others. He spun into action like a wheel in motion. He persuaded Penguin, the top mass-circulation publisher of the day, to bring out a book he would write called *Persecution 1961* to coincide with the opening of the campaign. He also asked Britain's leading liberal Sunday newspaper, the *Observer*, to give him the front page of its review section on launch day. They agreed. The article, which he would write, would be the single most important way of reaching the public.

Through the *Observer*, Benenson persuaded other leading papers around the world to carry the same article on the same day or shortly thereafter. Soon *Le Monde* in Paris, the *New York Herald Tribune*, the *Neue Zuricher Zeitung* in Switzerland, and about twenty other papers were in on the plan. Winning such access to the world's press would have been virtually impossible for a major statesman. It was an astounding feat for a young, little-known former lawyer.

"Prisoners of conscience"

Meanwhile, the group had reached some decisions. Amnesty would fight for "prisoners of conscience." It was Eric Baker's memorable phrase and it referred to people who were in prison or being persecuted for their ideas — writers, artists, musicians, or anyone else. The campaign would refuse to take up the cases of anyone who used or advocated violence. Naturally, tyrants and governments that abused human rights never admitted to doing so. They not only imprisoned or killed their victims, but also demeaned them by using

DISAPPEARED

labels like "criminals," "spies," "counter-revolutionaries," or "terrorists." The words "prisoners of conscience" had a poetic ring to them, cutting through to the truth of injustice. The phrase has long since passed into the political language of the world.

Many governments had signed impressive agreements and adopted international documents promising to respect human dignity. The United Nations Universal Declaration of Human Rights was one such document. But fine words were often no guarantee of fine deeds. Matching noble-sounding promises to real people in real, everyday situations was a different matter entirely. Benenson planned to

= DEAD ?

One of the most nightmarish tactics used by repressive governments is to arrest or kidnap opponents and then deny all knowledge of where the victims are held. The missing have often been tortured or murdered and their bodies buried secretly. Amnesty continues to campaign against this gross violation of human rights.

campaign for specific individuals who urgently needed the organization's help.

"Groups of Three"

Members of Amnesty also decided that the organization would be strictly neutral in political matters. It would simply take a stand for human decency against injustice. The organization would not get involved in ideological debates. To avoid favoritism and charges of bias, Benenson had the brilliantly simple idea of setting up "Groups of Three," small local groups that would adopt three prisoners from different parts of the divided world and devote equal time to each. One prisoner

"In a world full of cynicism and pessimism, Amnesty International is a beacon of hope. It is the proof that ordinary people have power. Thousands of men and women have been rescued from unfair imprisonment, torture and execution by the simple act of letter writing."

Peter Gabriel, musician

would be from the capitalist West, another from the communist East, and the last from somewhere in the Third World. No Amnesty group was allowed to pick a prisoner from its own country. This principle became a cornerstone of Amnesty's work in those early days.

To fight for their adopted prisoners, the Groups of Three would use the simplest of weapons. They would write polite letters addressed to the jailers, heads of governments, and embassies pleading for the prisoners' freedom. The reasoning behind this movement was not just that the basic act of writing letters could help to free the prisoners, but that the tide of public opinion which obviously stood behind these letters might. The idea that such a simple tactic could work against authoritarian governments seemed almost preposterous. But it was a stroke of genius. Anyone could take part in such a campaign, so it was a good way to get ordinary people involved in a massive group effort.

More important, this simple weapon would work. Governments and their officials were used to speaking to each other in the formal, restrained language of international diplomacy. They had never before faced floods of such letters from outraged citizens in other countries who politely, but directly, expressed their views. It was quite a new way of exerting moral pressure. Before long, Benenson's letters would open the doors of thousands of jails.

Candle in barbed wire

The campaign also needed a symbol — a logo. A picture of faces or hands behind bars was one powerful idea for an image. But a Chinese proverb, "Better to light a candle than curse the darkness," inspired an even more potent one. Benenson thought of a burning candle, symbolizing life and spirit, surrounded by barbed wire, signifying cruel imprisonment. He asked a young British artist, Diana Redhouse, to translate the idea onto paper, and she produced the beautifully simple but evocative symbol by which Amnesty International is now known.

The official campaign launch day for "Appeal for Amnesty, 1961" was coming nearer and nearer. Everything now depended on Benenson's article for the *Observer*.

"The Forgotten Prisoners"

The article had to be good, and it was. On Sunday, May 28, 1961, the paper's weekend review was dominated by a haunting image of a face behind wire, six photographs of incarcerated men, and the headline "The Forgotten Prisoners." A short paragraph explained: "On both sides of the Iron Curtain, thousands of men and women are being held in [jail] without trial because their political or religious views differ from those of their governments. Peter Benenson, a London lawyer, conceived the idea of a world campaign, 'Appeal for Amnesty, 1961,' to urge governments to release these people or at least give them a fair trial."

Benenson began: "Open your newspaper any day of the week and you will find a report from somewhere in the world of someone being imprisoned, tortured or executed because his opinions or religion are unacceptable to his government. There are several million such people in prison — by no means all of

Above: All over the world, many prisoners are kept in cramped, overcrowded conditions. Amnesty often asks that prisoners be allowed to see a doctor, lawyer, or relatives and that they be allowed to read, study, write letters, and get exercise.

Opposite: "Better to light a candle than curse the darkness." A Chinese proverb inspired the image of a candle in barbed wire that became the Amnesty symbol.

SIX POLITICAL PRISONERS : left, Constantin Noica, the philosopher, now in a Rumanian gaol; centre, the Rev. Ashton Jones, friend of the Negroes, recently in gaol in the United States; right, Agostino Neto, Angolan poet and doctor, held without trial by the Portuguese. Their cases are described in the article below.

Left, Archbishop Beran of Prague, held in custody by the Czechs; centre, Toni Ambatielos, the Greek Communist and trade unionist prisoner, whose wife is English; right Cardinal Mindszenty, Primate of Hungary, formerly a prisoner and now a political refugee trapped in the United States Embassy, Budapest.

ON BOTH SIDES of the Iron Curtain, thousands of men and women are being held in gaol without trial because their political or religious views differ from those of their Governments. Peter Benenson, a London lawyer, conceived the idea of a world campaign, APPEAL FOR AMNESTY, 1961, to urge Governments to release these people or at least give them a fair trial. The campaign opens to-day, and "The Observer" is glad to offer it a platform.

The Forgotten Prisoners

OPEN your newspaper any day of the week and you will find a report from somewhere in the world of someone being imprisoned, tortured or executed because his opinions or religion are unacceptable to his government. There are several million such people in prison—by no means all of them behind the Iron and Bamboo Curtains—and their numbers are growing. The newspaper reader feels a sickening sense of impotence. Yet if these feelings of disgust all over the world could be united into common action, something effective could be done.

In 1945 the founder members of the United Nations approved the Universal Declaration of Human Rights:—

There is a growing tendency all over the world to disguise the real grounds upon which "non-conformists" are imprisoned. In Spain, students who circulate leaflets calling for the right to hold discussions on current affairs are charged with "military rebellion." In Hungary, Catholic priests who have tried to keep their choir schools open have been charged with "homosexuality." These cover-up charges indicate that governments are by no means in-sensitive to the pressure of outside opinion. And when world opinion is concentrated on one weak spot, it can sometimes succeed in making a government relent. For instance, the Hungarian poet Tibor Dery was recently released after the formation of "Tibor Dery committees" in

[...columns continue...]

campaigns, which opens to-day, is the result of an initiative by a group of lawyers, writers and publishers. In London, who share the underlying conviction expressed by Voltaire: "I detest your views, but am pre-pared to die for your right to express them." We have set up an office in London to collect information about the names, numbers and conditions of what we have decided to call "Prisoners of Conscience," and we define them thus : "Any person who is physically restrained (by imprison-ment or otherwise) from expressing (in any form of words or symbols) any opinion which he honestly holds and which does not advocate or condone personal violence." We also exclude those who have conspired with a foreign government to over-

Amat, who tried to build a coalition of democratic groups, and has been in prison without trial since Nov-ember, 1958; and of two white men persecuted by their own race for preaching that the coloured races should have equal rights—Ashton Jones, the sixty-five-year-old minis-ter, who last year was repeatedly beaten-up and three times im-prisoned in Louisiana and Texas for doing what the Freedom Riders are now doing in Alabama ; and Patrick Duncan, the son of a former South African Governor-General, who, after three stays in prison, has just been served with an order forbidding him from attending or addressing any meeting for five years.

' Find out who is

out who is in gaol." This is hard advice to follow, because there are few governments which welcome inquiries about the number of Prisoners of Conscience they hold in prison. But another test of freedom one can apply is whether the Press is allowed to criticise the govern-ment. Even many democratic gov-ernments are surprisingly sensitive to Press criticism. In France, Gen-eral de Gaulle has intensified news-paper seizures, a policy he inherited from the Fourth Republic. In Britain and the United States occasional attempts are made to draw the sting of Press criticism by the technique of taking editors into confidence about a "security secret," as in the Blake spy case.

Within the British Common-

lawyer is able to present the defence in the way he thinks best. In recent years there has been a regrettable trend in some of these countries that take pride in possessing an inde-pendent judiciary: by declaring a state of emergency and taking their opponents into "preventive deten-tion," governments have side-stepped the need to make and prove criminal charges. At the other extreme there is the enthusiasm in Soviet countries to set up institutions which, though called courts, are really nothing of the sort. The so-called "comradely courts" in the U.S.S.R. which have power to deal with "parasites," are in essence little more than depart-ments of the Ministry of Labour, shifting "square pegs" into empty holes in Siberia. In China the trans-migration of labour by an allegedly judicial process is on a gigantic scale.

The most rapid way of bringing relief to Prisoners of Conscience is publicity, especially publicity among their fellow-citizens. With the pres-sure of emergent nationalism and the tensions of the Cold War, there are bound to be situations where governments are led to take emer-gency measures to protect their existence. It is vital that public opinion should insist that these measures should not be excessive, nor prolonged after the moment of danger. If the emergency is to last a long time, then a government should be induced to allow its opponents out of prison, to seek asylum abroad.

Frontier control more efficient

Although there are no statistics, it is likely that recent years have seen a steady decrease in the number of people reaching asylum. This is

willing to give out translation and correspondence work to refugees but no machinery to link supply with demand. Those regimes that refuse to allow their nationals to seek asylum on the ground that they go abroad only to conspire, might be less reluctant if they knew that, on arrival, the refugees would not be locking their hands in idle frustration.

The members of the Council of Europe have agreed a Convention in Human Rights, and set up a com-mission to secure its enforcement. Some countries have acceded to their citizens the right to approach the commission individually. By some, including Britain, have refused to accept the jurisdiction of the com-mission over individual complaints and France has refused to ratify the Convention at all. Public opinion should insist on the establishment of effective supra-national machinery: not only in Europe but on simi-lar lines in other continents.

This is an especially suitable year for an Amnesty Campaign. It is the centenary of President Lincoln's in-auguration, and of the beginning of the Civil War which ended with the liberation of the American slaves ; it is also the centenary of the decree that emancipated the Russian serfs. A hundred years ago Mr. Gladstone's budget swept away the oppressive duties on newsprint and so enlarges the range and freedom of the Press. 1861 marked the end of the tyranny of King "Bomba" of Naples, and the creation of a united Italy : it was also the year of the death of Lavoisier, the French Dominican oppo-nent of Bourbon and Orleanist oppression.

The success of the 1961 Amnesty Campaign depends on how sharply and powerfully it is possible to rally public opinion. It depends, too

---

Peter Benenson's Observer article launched the Amnesty movement in 1961. Benenson drew attention to the millions of individual men and women suffering for their beliefs and called for worldwide public protest to help prisoners of conscience.

them behind the Iron and Bamboo Curtains — and their numbers are growing. The newspaper reader feels a sickening sense of impotence. Yet if these feelings of disgust all over the world could be united into common action, something effective could be done."

All the blazing anger and sense of purpose that had driven Benenson for months was written into this article. It was a document calling on citizens around the world to unite in their common humanity and demand an immediate end to the abuses of tyranny.

A handful among many

Benenson gave faces and names to a handful of the multitude of suffering prisoners of conscience from very different countries all over the world. There was the Angolan poet and doctor, Agostino Neto, who had suffered "revolting brutality" at the hands of the ruling Portuguese authorities. He had been flogged in front of his family and dragged away to prison without a trial for the "crime" of trying to improve health care for his country. A Spanish lawyer, Antonio Amat, was imprisoned without trial for trying to form a pro-democracy group. József Cardinal Mindszenty of

Hungary and Archbishop Josef Beran of Prague, influential clerics from Communist Eastern Europe, had been imprisoned for opposing their governments. In the southern United States and in South Africa, white men had been imprisoned for helping blacks.

Benenson suggested a new way to end these outrages: "The most rapid way of bringing relief to prisoners of conscience is publicity, especially publicity among their fellow citizens." The success of the campaign would depend on how sharply and powerfully public opinion could be rallied and on the campaign "being all-embracing in its composition, international in its character and politically impartial. Any group is welcome to take part which is prepared to condemn persecution regardless of where it occurs, who is responsible or what are the ideas suppressed."

Reminding readers that it had been nearly one hundred years since Abraham Lincoln freed American slaves and the Russians abolished serfdom, Benenson concluded: "Experience shows that in matters such as these governments are prepared to follow only where public opinion leads. Pressure of opinion a hundred years ago brought about emancipation of the slaves. It is now for man to insist upon the same freedom for his mind as he has won for his body."

Amnesty is born

The public response to Benenson's article was astonishing. Over one thousand letters flooded in from the countries where the article had appeared. So, too, did donations and information on hundreds of other prisoners of conscience. Public reaction indicated that Amnesty needed immediate reorganization in order to properly accommodate these responses. The basement of Benenson's cramped offices at 1 Mitre Court became the headquarters. Amnesty would combine a tough-minded approach to detail with a flair for publicity to get its moral message across. The staff, all volunteers at first, worked wherever they could find a space — on chairs, on the tops of filing cabinets, on the floor. The scene looked chaotic. But the staff members were filled with a steely determination to get results.

Within weeks, the energy of the dedicated amateurs at Mitre Court had been duplicated by local groups

Two of the cases highlighted in the Observer *article: Above: Agostino Neto, the imprisoned Angolan poet and doctor, would later become president of his country.*

Below: Toni Ambatielos was a Greek communist and trade unionist.

springing up around the country. More volunteers helped to put the thousands of people who had written in after seeing the article in touch with each other. Local groups adopted prisoners of conscience and started to write letters to governments on their behalf.

The need for accurate information

But who were the prisoners of conscience? Where were they being held? What false crimes were they accused of? Why were they in prison? How could Amnesty help? The new campaigners — and the groups springing up all over Britain and in other parts of the world — desperately needed to know the answers to these questions.

A massive new network of information and intelligence was needed. In his *Observer* article, Benenson had estimated that there were millions of prisoners of conscience around the world. That figure was a guess. It may well have been accurate, but no one had any way of knowing for certain.

A research department needed to be set up immediately. Benenson turned to Christel Marsh, a prewar refugee from Nazi Germany. He asked her to find out everything about all the prisoners of conscience around the world. Benenson's instructions were vague: "Look through the newspapers," he suggested. "Use your initiative." But he communicated a sense of urgency and optimism.

Marsh started methodically. On a piece of paper, she wrote by hand the name of each country for which she had information. She listed the names of prisoners and any brief details concerning each case. By the end of the first day, she had assembled Amnesty's first research data base — a flimsy handful of paper.

The files grew rapidly with the help of a team of dedicated volunteers. Details of thousands of new cases came pouring in. Within a short time, Amnesty's "library," as the research department became known, would be a source of accurate, detailed information respected and trusted everywhere.

First success

Josef Beran, the Catholic archbishop of Prague, had survived two concentration camps during the Nazi

occupation. But in 1949, he was arrested again for delivering a sermon protesting the new Communist government that had seized power in a coup. In 1961, Beran had been in prison for twelve years.

With financial help from the London-based Catholic newspaper, the *Universe*, Amnesty sent one of its most prestigious members, respected human rights campaigner and former Irish foreign minister Sean MacBride, to Prague to see what he could do. The Czech prime minister refused to meet him, but MacBride managed to see the foreign minister. Beran's conditions were improved, but he was still kept in prison. Amnesty increased the pressure with letters, demonstrations, and telegrams demanding the archbishop's freedom. After little more than a year, the Czech government relented, releasing him first to house arrest in his palace and later letting him go to Rome. Archbishop Josef Beran's case was important because it proved beyond a doubt that Amnesty's methods could succeed even in Communist countries.

By 1964, Amnesty could claim many successes: in East Germany, a jailed trade unionist, Heinz Brandt, was freed after a two-year campaign; in Ghana, 152 opponents of the president had been released; and in Greece, Egypt, and Burma (now Myanmar), thousands were freed after Amnesty appeals.

The first two hundred letters

Benenson's belief in the power of simple letter-writing campaigns had been rewarded and, for a prisoner, the effect sometimes seemed miraculous. Years later, Julio de Penez Valdar, a trade union leader imprisoned naked in a dungeon in the Dominican Republic, described what happened when Amnesty members started sending letters to his jailers: "When the first two hundred letters came the guards gave me back my clothes. Then the next two hundred letters came and the prison director came to see me. When the next pile of letters arrived, the director got in touch with his superior. The letters kept coming and coming, three thousand of them. The President was informed. The letters kept arriving and the President called the prison to let me go. After I was released the President called me to his office for a man to man talk. He said: 'How

**amnesty
international**
défend les prisonniers d'opinion dans le
monde, lutte pour l'abolition
de la torture et de la peine de mort. *prix Nobel de la paix 1977*

A·M·N·I·S·T·I·A
I·N·T·E·R·N·A·C·I·O·N·A·L

SECCION CHILENA

Writing letters is still one of the most effective ways of putting pressure on a government. These are members of Amnesty's Japanese section.

is it that a trade union leader like you has so many friends all over the world?' He showed me an enormous box full of letters he had received and, when we parted, he gave them to me. I still have them."

Sean MacBride experienced an equally astounding reaction when he visited Romania in 1964. The country's justice minister had been confused when, out of the blue, he started to receive letters from ordinary people all around the world about some of the men and women in his prisons. Romania was an isolated Eastern bloc country, and the protests had made the minister wonder why his prisoners had suddenly become famous. He sent an official to check their cases, decided there was no particular reason to keep them in jail, and simply set thousands of prisoners free.

Amnesty goes international
Peter Benenson, now aged forty, visited many places in Britain and Europe to set up Amnesty groups. By the end of the first year there were thirty-one groups in Britain. The first group in another country was set up

in West Germany, and Holland, Switzerland, Italy, and France followed. In 1962, other Amnesty groups were founded in Norway, Sweden, and Denmark. Later that year, after a conference in Belgium, all the groups decided to set up a permanent international organization to be called Amnesty International.

Sean MacBride became Amnesty International's chairman. The great philosopher Bertrand Russell was an ardent supporter, as were idealistic university students all through Europe who gave Amnesty much of its energy. Throughout this period, Benenson continued to act like a one-man whirlwind, bursting with ideas, infusing others with his enthusiasm.

The Haitian painter

As Amnesty grew, Benenson continued to have a hand in everything from finances to organization. Often, this was too much for one person. The finances were a little chaotic and sometimes prevented the group from doing as much as it wanted. But Benenson spent much of the money he had earned as a lawyer and some he had inherited from his father on the organization. He cared deeply about each of the prisoners Amnesty adopted and, perhaps inevitably, the physical stress and the emotional strain of the work began to affect his health. He tired easily and suffered from mysterious stomach pains and headaches.

Despite his poor health, he also carried out research missions to Lebanon, Egypt, Portugal, and elsewhere. One famous trip in 1964 was to Haiti, then ruled by the dictator François Duvalier, known as "Papa Doc." It was a difficult country to get into; the Haitian government was suspicious of foreigners. But Papa Doc was proud of his country's folk art, so Benenson decided to pose as a British folk artist on a visit to see Haitian arts and crafts. This masquerade was not very difficult for Benenson, since he painted as a hobby. To keep up the deception, he woke up before dawn each morning in his hotel room, made a few sketches of scenery outside the window, and left the results on the outside balcony.

His real work started after breakfast when he left the hotel. He met Haitian dissidents and recruited a network of people around the country who were able to

Amnesty International's founder, Peter Benenson.

27

give Amnesty accurate information about the human rights situation in Haiti for years to come. Benenson made sure he wasn't followed, and if the feared secret police visited his room, the pictures on his easel convinced them that his pose as an artist was genuine!

When he returned home, Benenson wrote a scathing report of Haiti's record of imprisonment and torture for the French newspaper *Le Monde*, which published it in a double-page spread. Furious, Papa Doc retaliated by expelling all British, French, and United States diplomats from the country.

Illness and withdrawal

By the mid-1960s, Amnesty had become a small but highly successful — and permanent — organization worldwide. Its networks and support groups grew, and it became more skillful at exerting moral pressure to help prisoners. Its representatives now enjoyed international respect. It also had experience with controversy when a British Amnesty group adopted the jailed black South African leader Nelson Mandela. The group was ordered to stop because Mandela had helped organize Umkhonto we Sizwe, or "Spear of the Nation," a violent paramilitary group.

But not everything was running smoothly. Benenson's personal commitment and energetic approach had helped to establish Amnesty on an international basis. But he had never had much time for administrative details and, more important, he was becoming exhausted. Some members complained that Amnesty was too heavily influenced by Benenson. There were arguments with colleagues as the organization's international and internal affairs became more and more complicated.

Meanwhile, Benenson's health was steadily declining. He had had intense stomach pain and blinding headaches for several years. The condition was crippling, and it was getting worse. His doctors were baffled. The strain of running Amnesty and the stress of emotional involvement in so many cases seemed to be making him ill. Benenson was physically and emotionally drained, and his colleagues wondered how he could continue to work. His condition did not improve in the months ahead.

Amnesty refuses to adopt political prisoners who advocate violence as prisoners of conscience. This rule applied to black South African leader Nelson Mandela, who spent nearly twenty-eight years in jail because of his commitment to "armed struggle" against apartheid.

In March 1967, Benenson withdrew from the organization. He had already decided that he did not want to run Amnesty for the rest of his life. "All I wished to do was to put the ship out to sea," he said later. His friend Eric Baker took over the management of the organization, and Benenson, aged forty-five, ended his day-to-day involvement with Amnesty.

Benenson's illness was diagnosed as celiac disease, a type of food allergy that could be treated easily once the doctors knew what it was. When Benenson recovered, he devoted much of his time to a farm he had bought, to his private world of prayer, to writing, and to a host of new ideas for other projects.

Amnesty continued to follow Benenson's principles. He remains to this day a much-loved and respected figure among its staff and volunteers. Through his example, his ideas, and the organization he founded, the principles he fought for now exert a greater influence than ever.

In the years that followed, Amnesty moved away from its small beginnings and grew immensely, winning support on every continent and becoming a truly international organization. From June 1967 to June 1968 the number of groups increased from 410 to 550.

Amnesty represented men and women tortured in Greece or Iran, abused in psychiatric hospitals in the Soviet Union, imprisoned in Indonesia or Afghanistan, or killed in Uganda, Guatemala, or Cambodia. It adopted and campaigned for poets, politicians, trade unionists, and teachers. Famous names on Amnesty's files during this period included the jailed playwright and future president of Czechoslovakia, Vaclav Havel, and Andrei Sakharov, the Soviet physicist and human rights campaigner who had become a prisoner of the Soviet labor camp system called the Gulag.

Amnesty groups directly helped thousands of prisoners around the world. Thousands more benefited indirectly from its work when Amnesty's concerns began to be taken up by government leaders, especially United States president Jimmy Carter.

Across the oceans

Amnesty's activities reflected a universal willingness to help from Europe into Africa, Asia, Latin America,

Peter Benenson gave up his day-to-day involvement with Amnesty in 1967, but he has continued to be a revered and respected figure in the movement. Here, he addresses an Amnesty meeting in Canada in 1986.

and Eastern Europe. Its members and organizations received gratitude and appreciation in return for their concerned efforts.

Two cases from Uruguay illustrate this beautifully. Lilian Celiberti, a Uruguayan woman living in exile in Brazil, was kidnapped in her home by Uruguayan security agents. They smuggled her across the border back into Uruguay, and she was charged with trying to enter the country secretly with subversive literature. Her two children, Camilo, eight, and Francesca, three, were abducted with her. In jail, she was tortured and told she would never see her children again. She signed a false confession so that they would be released, but she was sent to prison by a military court.

Amnesty International adopted Celiberti as a prisoner of conscience and her case was given to an Amnesty group in Italy. For the next five years, the Italian group worked ceaselessly on her behalf. They sent six hundred appeals and letters to the Uruguayan authorities and did not receive a single reply. They persuaded Italian politicians to take up the case. Questions were asked in the Italian and European parliaments, and Italian television broadcast news about the case. At the group's request, Italian delegations to Uruguay raised Lilian's case with their hosts. Italian lawyers wrote to the president of Uruguay's Supreme Military Tribunal. The group also wrote to Lilian's parents and raised money for her children so that they could visit her regularly in prison. In November 1983, Lilian Celiberti was released.

Lilian Celiberti wrote to the Amnesty group in Italy: "You have been present during all these years with a constancy and dedication which has accompanied me in the worst moments giving me strength and joy. I remember clearly the emotion I felt on returning to my cell after one of the fortnightly visits, the only time I talked to anyone, having learned about your letters. The solidarity that is expressed over oceans of distance gives strength and faith in one's solitude and helps one confront the repressive apparatus by keeping one's human integrity and its essential values intact."

Another Uruguayan, trade union leader Batlle Oxandabarat Scarrone, clashed with the authorities while trying to do his job. He marched with sugarcane cutters from the north of the country demanding better wages and working conditions and became president of a branch of Uruguay's union confederation, the Confederación Nacional de Trabajadores. He was arrested because of this in June 1972 and jailed for thirteen years.

An Amnesty International group in West Germany took up his case. Dedicated volunteers spent many hours writing letters, calling for his release, and giving moral support to Scarrone and his family. When he was released, they paid for his airfare to Spain, where his family now lived.

Scarrone wrote to thank the group: "There is no distance, no place or race which can stop human relationships being developed. . . . All we have to do is to think and be aware that there are millions of others . . . and that one can be of use to a fellow human being from a distance. To receive the word 'brother' and 'friend' comforts us and gives us the strength to go on with our principles to construct a more just and humane world. Today, happily, in freedom and in Spain with my family, censorship cannot prevent me from communicating my gratitude for everything you have done for me."

Above: Argentina, 1983. Families of some of the thousands of missing victims of the military dictatorship of the 1970s and early 1980s demonstrate in the capital, Buenos Aires.

Opposite: Guatemala in the 1980s. Top: Files of citizens targeted for assassination found in the interior minister's house in 1982. Bottom: Relatives of missing persons demonstrate to demand information about their sons, daughters, husbands, wives, mothers, and fathers.

ent de la partie de leuesque mais ilz turent al
les tost deliures de puson par paiant vne grãt
some dargent. De la mort du maistre du tem
ple.

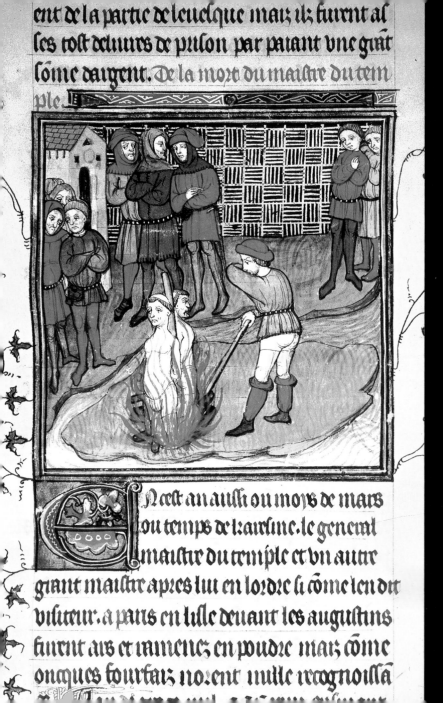

N cest an aussi ou mops de mars
ou temps de karesine. le general
maistre du temple et vn autre
giant maistre apres lui en lordre si come len dit
visiteur. a paris en lisle deuant les augustins
turent ars et ramenez en poudre mais come
onques sourfaiz noient nulle recognoissa

The Nobel Peace Prize

By the time Amnesty International was awarded the Nobel Peace Prize for 1977, it had earned a solid reputation for accuracy, dedication, and hard work. At the presentation ceremony, Amnesty's speaker defined the movement as "everyone who has ever written a letter asking for the release of a prisoner of conscience, everyone who has ever stood in a vigil mourning the death of a political prisoner, everyone who has ever handed out leaflets, stuffed envelopes, done the accounts. Every name on every petition counts."

Amnesty's campaigns have shed light on abuses in almost every country. In Benenson's words, "There is no area of the world where people are not suffering for their beliefs and no ideology which is blameless."

Amnesty International's reasons for existence are clear. Its basic principles oppose cruel, inhuman, or degrading treatment of any prisoners and demand fair and speedy trials for political prisoners. It calls for the immediate release of all prisoners of conscience — those detained because of their beliefs, religion, language, race, sex, or ethnic origin. In the organization's early years, most efforts were focused on prisoners of conscience. But Amnesty has also spoken out on other vital issues, such as the use of torture and the death penalty.

Torture — an epidemic

Amnesty's research uncovered the grisly fact that many governments still use torture. By the 1970s, as one Amnesty report stated, it was clear that "the torture of political prisoners is spreading like an epidemic throughout the world." The report detailed torture in thirty-two countries, including Vietnam, Greece, Brazil, the Soviet Union, Iran, South Africa, Turkey, and Indonesia. In 1990, despite some success in Amnesty's battle against this epidemic, the organization's researchers estimated that almost a third of the world's governments systematically used some kind of torture against their opponents.

Savage cruelty used by the powerful against the weak has long been a blot on human civilization. By perverting the latest technology, regimes in the modern world have developed terrible new methods to assume

Opposite: Killing or torturing people for their beliefs is nothing new; in medieval Europe, people were regularly burned alive for dissenting opinions. But in recent times, government-inspired savagery has reached epidemic proportions in some parts of the world.

Below: Skulls of Cambodians murdered by the Khmer Rouge lay throughout the countryside during the genocide of the late 1970s. The slaughter of hundreds of thousands of men, women, and children in the "killing fields" was one of the most savage abuses of human rights in modern times.

Opposite: The "ultimate human corruption." Top: The Spanish Inquisition four hundred years ago. Bottom: Public beating of suspected thieves in Jean-Bedel Bokassa's Central African Empire in the 1970s. Victims laid out on tables were beaten by soldiers and the emperor himself. Three men died of their injuries.

and maintain power. Some of these practices include electric shocks, mind-altering drugs, and sophisticated psychological methods of destroying personalities and the will to resist. Many of the older methods of torture are still used, in addition to newer ones. Victims may be forced to stay awake for many days at a time; or be forced with dozens of others into overcrowded cells for long periods without toilets; or beaten on the soles of their feet; or forced to watch while their wives, husbands, or even children are tortured in front of them.

Some governments have traded information on the most "effective" techniques and trained each other's torturers. For instance, Amnesty received information about a "school" for torturers run by the French in Algeria in 1959. Ten years later, the same techniques were being used in Brazil.

The ultimate corruption

Torture is often used to extract false confessions. But it is also a horrifying and absolute use of power by the state against an individual. Many brutal governments see torture simply as a useful tool for controlling their populations. As Amnesty puts it: "Torture humiliates the victim and dehumanizes the torturer. It is one of the ultimate human corruptions."

Torture is outlawed under international law. The International Covenant on Civil and Political Rights declares: "No one shall be subjected to torture or to cruel, inhuman or degrading treatment or punishment." But sometimes even countries with excellent human rights records, like Austria and Norway, ignore such declarations or agreements, even when they have signed them and agreed to the terms.

Amnesty tries to alert world public opinion to the desperate plight of torture victims in an effort to stop this savagery. In 1972, Amnesty set up conferences, published a series of reports, and organized a petition in 530 languages which was signed by more than one million people.

In the early 1980s, the campaign was intensified and Amnesty published a new report on world torture. It drew up a twelve-point plan to abolish torture and demanded that torturers be prosecuted for their deeds. Furthermore, any evidence obtained by torture was to

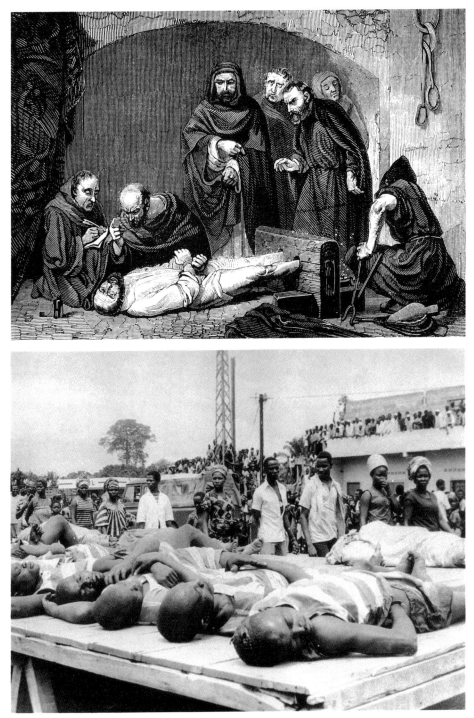

As Amnesty International grew, Peter Benenson's administrative duties took up an increasingly larger portion of his time.

be banned. In one successful case, relatives of a victim in Paraguay sued a police chief responsible for the torture. The court declared that "the torturer has become, like the pirate and slave trader before him . . . an enemy of all mankind."

"The most premeditated of murders"

Another Amnesty crusade has been against the death penalty. Both Peter Benenson's and Amnesty's founding statements had said that the organization strongly opposed executions. They believed that executions were a cold-blooded and cruel way to destroy a human life. But putting men, women, or even children to death has long been a punishment for certain crimes and political reasons. Many different and horrible methods have been used. All of them have been cruel. The terror and mental agony of a man or woman awaiting execution can scarcely be imagined.

The French writer and philosopher Albert Camus described the death penalty as "the most premeditated of murders." He believed that no criminal's deed, however calculated, could compare to its cruelty. He wrote: "For there to be an equivalence, the death penalty would have to punish a criminal who had warned his victim of the date at which he would inflict a horrible death on him and who, from that moment onward, had confined him at his mercy for months. Such a monster is not encountered in private life."

The countless victims of this brutal practice have included the Greek philosopher Socrates, large numbers of Christian saints, kings and queens like Charles I and Marie Antoinette, and most of the leaders of the French and Russian revolutions.

In the eighteenth century, mass executions in many countries of Europe were regarded as a form of entertainment. Even children could be hanged for minor crimes like stealing a loaf of bread. But things had changed by the late twentieth century. In Western Europe, widespread revulsion had followed the mass murders committed by dictators like Joseph Stalin and Adolf Hitler and the horrors of World War II when the Nazis had put millions of innocent people to death. Since then, the number of executions has fallen sharply, and a growing number of countries have abolished the death penalty. But in 1989, Amnesty International statistics showed that one hundred countries still retained the death penalty as a form of punishment.

"Cruel, inhuman and degrading"

There was a debate among Amnesty's members about whether the movement should campaign actively against this form of punishment. Some people wondered if Amnesty's scarce resources should be used to help victims of capital punishment (many of them murderers) when there might be more deserving people and causes. But at a special conference in Stockholm in 1977, Amnesty declared the death penalty "the ultimate cruel, inhuman and degrading punishment" that

Amnesty International sees the death penalty as "the ultimate cruel, inhuman and degrading punishment." This picture is from the film The Executioner's Song.

*Each Amnesty group champions three victims — one from a Western democracy, another from a Communist state, and the third from a developing country. We have followed the same principle in highlighting just three examples of Amnesty's work — first, the death penalty in the United States, then the human rights abuses across China, and, finall'' the terror in the dictatorship of Iraq.

"violates the right to life." Since then, Amnesty has been totally opposed to all forms of execution in all circumstances and has campaigned tirelessly against the use of the death penalty in every case it can. Amnesty appeals for clemency in individual cases by sending telegrams, faxes, and letters urging reprieves, and asking that sentences be set aside or commuted to terms of imprisonment.

Death in the United States*

In 1977, the United States' first execution in ten years took place. Ironically, this was also the year that

The death penalty is about to be administered in Uganda in 1973. Tied to a tree and naked under his canvas apron, an alleged guerrilla awaits execution by firing squad. The soldier on the right holds the black hood that will be put over the victim's head.

Amnesty launched its full campaign against the death penalty. It was a bizarre case. A double murderer named Gary Gilmore demanded to be put to death rather than face a life in prison. After a long legal battle — in the glare of worldwide media attention — Gilmore got his wish and was shot by a firing squad in Utah.

Gilmore's death was the result of a 1976 decision by the U.S. Supreme Court to permit executions. In 1972, the court had ruled against death penalty laws of the time as "cruel and unusual punishment." But this reversal ushered in a new era during which other states began to execute their death-row inmates. Prisoners have been shot, electrocuted, gassed, or killed by lethal injection in American prisons ever since. Executions are now running at the rate of up to twenty-five a year.

In many other ways, the United States has a good human rights record. And its record on executions is certainly far better than countries such as Iran, Thailand, or China, which carry out hundreds of executions each year. These are often in public and not only for murder, but also for a wide range of lesser crimes as well as political offenses.

"Amnesty has a credibility with the media, with [lawmakers], and with public opinion, that, it is fair to say, is as strong and as wide-reaching as that of any other international organization, with the possible exception of the Red Cross and UNICEF."
Jonathan Power,
in Amnesty International:
The Human Rights Story

Death row
There are now more than two thousand American men and women on "death row," awaiting their turns to be executed if the legal appeals against their sentences fail. The system often seems weighted against the poor, the badly educated, and people of ethnic minorities. The majority of those who have been put to death have, in fact, been from these three groups.

Despite protests, particularly from Amnesty, even teenagers who commit capital offenses have sometimes been put to death. There are only six countries in the world where this is still allowed. Appeals by Amnesty and others have led to executions being stopped by the courts in some cases. In 1988, two American fifteen-year-olds, Paula Cooper and William Wayne Thompson, were reprieved in this way.

The case of Shabaka Waglimi
In Florida, Shabaka Waglimi was sentenced to death for crimes he had not committed. He had set out with another man to commit an armed robbery. Shabaka

was a hopeless criminal. But this time, the woman he intended to rob reminded him of his mother, and he abandoned the attempt halfway through. Overcome by shame and remorse, he went to a police station the next day and gave himself up. However, on the same night as the failed robbery, another woman had been raped, robbed, and murdered.

The police charged Shabaka for these crimes. At his trial, he was the only black man in the courtroom. His lawyer was a young graduate who had never conducted a criminal case before and who didn't even realize Shabaka was being tried for murder. Shabaka was convicted of murder, rape, and robbery by an all-white jury on July 3, 1974, and sentenced to death.

Shabaka's death watch

Like other death-row inmates, Shabaka was kept completely alone in a cell eight feet (2.4 m) long

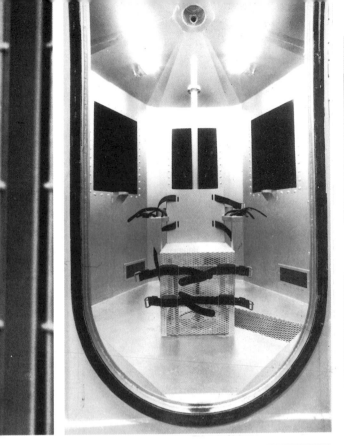

Above left: The gas chamber in a Maryland penitentiary. Above right: The gallows at Washington State Penitentiary in Walla Walla. Most U.S. executions are now carried out by electrocution or lethal injection. Left: Many "death row" inmates are black and poor.

twenty-four hours a day. Twice a week he was escorted outside for two hours of exercise. Showers were allowed once every two days, but he was searched afterward to make sure that he had smuggled nothing back to his cell.

In every country, whatever the method of killing, the countdown to a condemned person's death is a horrible ritual. It was no different for Shabaka, who waited for the electric chair in Florida.

In October 1983, Shabaka heard that his death warrant had been signed. He was moved to the death watch cell — exactly thirty feet (9 m) from the electric chair, which he could see being tested twice a day. The horrifying countdown to his death began. He was measured for his death suit and a death certificate was prepared in advance, giving the cause of death as "legal execution by electrocution." But Shabaka had always insisted he was innocent and, with fifteen hours to go, his prayers were answered. His lawyer had won a stay of execution.

In 1986, Shabaka was granted a new trial and the evidence against him proved false. He was finally released. His ordeal had lasted fourteen years. Amnesty had been prominent in the campaign to save Shabaka's life. Now he joined Amnesty's campaign against the death penalty.

China's shame

On the other side of the globe from the United States is the People's Republic of China. This Communist country has long had a terrible record of using the death penalty, torture, and political imprisonment. Amnesty has fought against all these abuses since its inception. During the 1980s, for instance, Amnesty protested and appealed for an end to hundreds of executions taking place as part of a government crackdown. Prisoners were shot, sometimes at mass executions, not only for murder but also for theft and bribery. Before their deaths, the victims were often publicly humiliated at "mass sentencing" rallies or paraded in the streets.

Few detailed eyewitness accounts of these horrors usually reach the outside world. But in 1983, Amnesty received this nightmarish description of an execution outside the city of Zhengzhou: "The forty-five prisoners

were led to a row of forty-five wooden stakes; some had lost the use of their legs through fear and had to be dragged to the stakes. Forty-five police officers aimed rifles at the prisoners' heads and shot them all at once at close range. Bodies which lay quivering on the ground were shot again. After the executions, the crowd watching from the banks of the creek bed surged down from the banks and closed in, shouting. The front rows broke through the police line to where the bodies

An all-night vigil protests an execution in South Carolina. Many Americans, including those of the United States' Amnesty section, strongly oppose the death penalty.

lay, and stopped short in horror as they got near enough to make out details. But the pressure behind them was too great; many [people] were pushed ahead and forced to trample the bodies. Some fell sprawling over them. . . . To protect the bodies, a policeman pulled out one of the numbered stakes, scooped up some brains on the circular sign, and held people at bay with it."

China has been through many bloody political upheavals. It is estimated that huge numbers of people died in the terror of Chairman Mao Tse-tung's Cultural Revolution in the 1960s. Intellectuals were forced to do farm work in the countryside. Millions were sent to work camps, and dissent was furiously suppressed. After Mao's death in 1976, the system became a little more lenient. But in a famous 1978 report, Amnesty revealed that political imprisonment remained widespread and that many people were still being put to death for their views.

Free after thirty years

One prisoner of conscience adopted by Amnesty at this time was Wei Jingsheng, one of the leaders of a pro-democracy movement. He published a magazine that criticized the Communist system and called for human rights. He was put on trial in 1979 in Beijing for conducting "counter-revolutionary propaganda and agitation" and for supposedly passing military secrets to a foreigner. Prisoners who have been found guilty in China often have their heads shaved. But Wei's head was shaved before his trial even started — his guilt had been decided in advance. Wei was sentenced to fifteen years in prison.

Five years later, Amnesty received alarming news about Jingsheng. As a result of his spending long periods of time in solitary confinement, Wei's mental health had collapsed, and he was being treated for a personality disorder called schizophrenia. In 1988, he was still in prison, and his condition was being kept secret. When the Norwegian prime minister visited China that year, at Amnesty's request, he raised Wei's case with Chinese leaders.

Peter Benenson wrote in 1961 that "it is impossible to know even to the nearest million how many Chinese are today suffering imprisonment for their opinions."

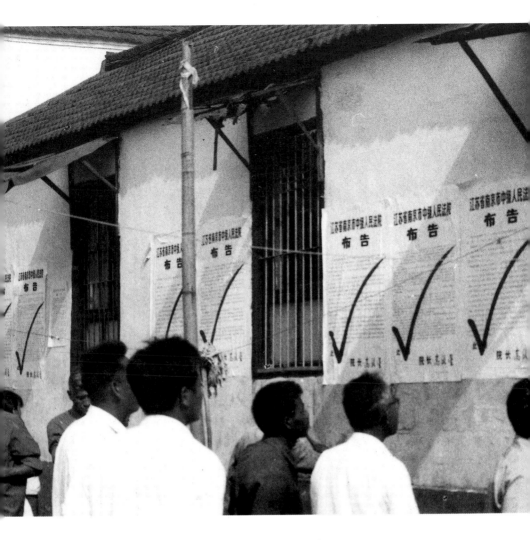

His words are equally relevant today. For over three decades, Amnesty's researchers, members, and officials have been kept depressingly busy by the Chinese Communist authorities.

Other prisoners from around the world who were adopted and defended by Amnesty have also obtained their release. Several leading Chinese Catholic priests were set free in the late 1980s following pressure from Amnesty groups in Europe. In May 1988, Father Thomas You Guojie, who had been either in prison or a work camp since 1957, was released. Another prisoner of conscience, Father Stanislas Yan, had spent

Posters list the names of people sentenced to death in China. The large checks mean that the sentences have been carried out. Often, victims are publicly humiliated at mass-sentencing rallies before being shot.

thirty years in jail or a work camp. Father Yan was adopted by a French Amnesty group and was eventually freed in 1987.

Also in 1987, Amnesty published a report giving details of the "persistent and widespread" use of torture in China despite government efforts to stop it. Prisoners had been whipped, hung by their arms, and assaulted with electric batons to extract confessions. In one city, Baoshan, police tortured one hundred suspects over two cases of theft. Two of the victims died, and a third committed suicide. Prisoners were psychologically tortured by years of solitary confinement, unable to speak to their families or fellow prisoners.

Tiananmen Square

The brutal side of China had been chronicled by Amnesty for some years before the events of June 3, 1989. Yet for many months, China had seemed a more open and relaxed country than it had for years. To the outside world, its friendly image was of tourists having their photographs taken on the Great Wall.

In April, a small number of students demonstrated peacefully in the heart of Beijing for political reforms and an end to official corruption. To everyone's surprise, the authorities did nothing to stop them. Soon the small demonstrations became a vast popular movement for democracy and a free press. Huge, gentle crowds calling for democracy gathered in Tiananmen Square day after day beneath a huge portrait of Chairman Mao. The authorities were not sure what to do about this challenge.

In May, students began a hunger strike and asked for talks with Communist party leaders. As the astonished world watched the drama unfold on live television, a million people filled the square each day to support the students. The first soldiers sent to clear the square found themselves peacefully disarmed by the crowds. Some even joined the demonstrations.

On the night of June 3, the students' dream turned into a nightmare. By now the demonstrations had become smaller. Communist party leader Deng Xiaoping ordered new soldiers from a remote province into Beijing with tanks. They entered Tiananmen Square, firing rifles and machine guns into the unarmed crowds. Amnesty later estimated that a thousand demonstrators were massacred in that onslaught, some crushed to death by tanks as they huddled in tents.

The full force of state repression snapped back into place. Chinese newspapers, which had begun to report the truth, were suddenly full of propaganda again. The world television reports were stopped by Chinese authorities as suddenly as they had begun. Once more, Amnesty International began the task of documenting a new wave of secret trials, political imprisonments, and executions as the government persecuted those who had supported the students. And Amnesty officials and groups around the world again took up the long, slow task of campaigning to end repression.

Iraqi terror: a case history

Examples of almost all the types of oppression which Amnesty has ever campaigned against could still be found in horrifying abundance in Iraq in the 1990s.

At a candle-lighting ceremony in London in 1981 marking Amnesty's twentieth anniversary, Benenson had observed: "The candle burns not for us, but for all those whom we failed to rescue, who were shot on the way to prison, who were tortured, who were kidnapped, who 'disappeared.' That's what the candle is for."

Those words could well serve for the whole Iraqi people, who were in the grip of one of the modern world's most brutal regimes. President Saddam Hussein's rule was based on a policy of terror. Dissent of any kind was forbidden. The feared secret police and their informers were everywhere, ready to punish dissent of any kind. Torture was routine, and hundreds of people faced execution each year.

Mass executions, mass deportations, and public killings took place often in Iraq. Even groups of children were publicly executed. Anyone heard criticizing either the president or his ruling Ba'ath party would be tortured or executed or both. Like two other mass killers of this century, Adolf Hitler and Joseph Stalin, Saddam Hussein even killed some of his closest political allies and military commanders because he feared that they might become rivals.

The regime was so brutal that Amnesty decided it was too dangerous to adopt individual prisoners of

"Governments that are criticized denounce Amnesty, but even though they have been given an Amnesty report a month or two before it is due to be published, they rarely try to put the record straight."
Jonathan Power, in Amnesty International: The Human Rights Story

47

conscience inside Iraq. The organization's members feared that such support might make a prisoner's situation even worse. Instead, Amnesty tried to alert the world to Iraqi abuses by publishing reports and drawing attention to the horrors committed there.

The "Butcher of Baghdad"

Saddam Hussein, nicknamed "the Butcher of Baghdad," was said to have killed his first political opponent at the age of fourteen. Two weeks after taking power in 1979, he ordered the deaths of twenty-two former colleagues, including members of the ruling Revolutionary Command Council. After an attempted coup, he forced senior officials and army officers to join him as members of the firing squad. In 1983, he reportedly shot and killed a minister in his cabinet who criticized him.

Left: Savage repression followed the massacre in Beijing's Tiananmen Square. Government-run television showed prodemocracy students and workers who had taken part in the demonstrations being given brief trials and sentenced to death.

Saddam Hussein initiated a bloody nine-year war by invading the neighboring country of Iran in September 1980. He broke international law and a military taboo which had lasted since World War I by using poison gas as a weapon on the battlefield. Hussein later used poison gas again to massacre five thousand of his own people. This horrible action was part of a long, cruel campaign to destroy the identity of Kurdish people who occupy northeastern Iraq.

On August 2, 1990, Iraqi forces crossed the border into Kuwait and assumed military control of that country. Saddam Hussein declared that there was now no such country as Kuwait. Eyewitnesses reported killings and imprisonment of Kuwaiti citizens. Foreign nationals were either detained and then released, or were detained in the country as political hostages. Other eyewitnesses reported the seizing of food, water, and medical equipment by Iraqi soldiers. Many of these eyewitnesses fled across the desert in desperate attempts to escape the brutal takeover.

In addition to holding foreign hostages, Hussein's Iraq had secret "revolutionary courts" which staged brief summary trials and handed out death sentences against which there was no appeal. Some laws were even kept secret, so people — foreign and otherwise — could be punished for "crimes" they didn't even know existed. It was painfully obvious that human rights abuses were rampant in this troubled nation.

Suffer the little children

But perhaps the most horrifying reports were allegations of systematic torture. This included the torture of young children and whole families. One former political prisoner told Amnesty what happened to his family: "My mother, who was seventy-three, three sisters and three brothers with five children aged between five and thirteen were arrested and brought in front of me. They were subjected to [beatings] on the soles of the feet and electric shocks." He also described what happened to babies in the prison. "Usually they keep such children in a separate cell next to the mother's or father's cell and deprive them of milk in order to force the parents to confess. I saw a five-month-old baby screaming in this state."

Amnesty members in Sweden march to protest against torture, executions, and disappearances.

In 1989, Amnesty ran a worldwide crusade protesting human rights abuses against Kurdish children by the Iraqi government. At the United Nations Human Rights Commission that year, Iraq used its political influence to escape detailed examination of its appalling record. But an Amnesty report concluded: "Brutal treatment of children has become routine in the prisons of Iraq." Children have been tortured, executed, assassinated, arrested, and held without trial or have "disappeared," presumably killed. In March 1986, fifteen schoolchildren and students in the city of Arbil were rounded up and summarily executed in public in retaliation for the wounding of a government official.

The Iraqi government would also poison people it considered enemies. Thallium compound, a slow-acting rat poison, was commonly used. One victim was a fourteen-year-old Kurdish girl, Trifa Said Muhammad. She and her family were in the house of a member of a banned Kurdish group when they drank a yogurt drink that had been laced with the powerful thallium poison. Trifa's grandmother and two others died. There was vomiting, high fever, and paralysis. Trifa's hair fell out, and she had terrible pains in her legs. After three weeks, she could not walk. Suffering dreadfully, she escaped by donkey to Iran. She was then flown to Holland for treatment, not knowing whether she would be able to use her legs again.

Amnesty had drawn attention to human rights violations in Iraq for years. But for a long time, Western governments supported Saddam Hussein with weapons, technology, and trade. This is because they were more worried about Iraq's main enemy, Iran, another country with a deplorable human rights record.

"The worldwide human-rights movement has made significant improvements in the past, and it can make more of them in the future. . . . Now the momentum must increase. It all begins with individual people caring, then doing something to help individual people in need."
John G. Healey, executive director of Amnesty International U.S.A.

Amnesty's changing role

Over the years, Amnesty's principles have not changed, but its tasks have. Amnesty's help is needed wherever oppression breaks out. Even a brief glance through collections of old newspapers reveals that the global pattern of oppression changes. Amnesty's files provide a more detailed picture, like satellite photographs of huge locust plagues or hurricanes seen from space.

In the late 1950s and early 1960s, for example, Spain was a major abuser of human rights. Today, its

Above and right: Kurdish villagers were murdered by Iraqi poison gas in Halabja in 1988. The massacre of four thousand people was part of Iraqi president Saddam Hussein's long reign of terror, torture, and murder against his opponents. Amnesty tried in vain to draw attention to Iraq's horrific human rights record for years before Saddam Hussein's invasion of Kuwait in 1990.

record is infinitely improved, and it is a parliamentary democracy. In the 1950s and 1960s, Cambodia barely registered as one of the world's trouble spots. But by the late 1970s, American bombing during the Vietnam War was followed by four years of genocide as a group of Cambodian communists called the Khmer Rouge murdered hundreds of thousands of fellow Cambodians in the name of a Marxist revolution. In the mid-1980s, Argentina became a democracy. Up to that time, it had had one of the world's worst human rights records. The government had kidnapped and secretly murdered thousands of opponents in the "dirty war" of the 1970s. The Soviet Union, where an entire system had been built on secret police, concentration camps, and mass murder, has changed beyond recognition. In 1989, largely peaceful revolutions displaced the Communist tyranny of Eastern Europe that had long figured prominently in Amnesty's work.

Peter Benenson's ideas and Amnesty's dedicated work should perhaps be given some credit for these positive changes. Amnesty's unceasing efforts have probably done much to change the climate of political and moral opinion around the world, to demand basic human rights for all individuals, and to put an end to the abuses of tyranny.

"The nonviolent approach does not immediately change the heart of the oppressor. It first does something to the hearts and souls of those committed to it. It gives them new self-respect; it calls up resources of strength and courage that they did not know they had. Finally it reaches the opponent and so stirs his conscience that reconciliation becomes a reality."
Martin Luther King, Jr.

Even after his resignation, Peter Benenson remained active in the affairs of Amnesty International.

The worldwide crusade

Thirty years after the start of Peter Benenson's one-man crusade, Amnesty has grown into the world's largest and most respected human rights movement. Seven hundred thousand members in 150 countries with over four thousand separate local volunteer groups in seventy countries are working steadily for the release of prisoners. From the two rooms in Benenson's basement, Amnesty has become one of the most respected and effective human rights organizations in the world.

In 1961, the cases of over 34,000 prisoners of conscience were taken up by Amnesty. By 1990, 28,937 of these had been closed. Its most extraordinary supporters have been in countries with a record of persecution and oppression. An Amnesty activist in a democratic and open country is hardly likely to land in trouble with the authorities. The same activity in a

country run by a dictator with a secret police system demands great bravery.

Yet, even in the 1990s, Amnesty International remains an essentially simple movement. Its activists are motivated by the same deeply felt emotional experience that moved Peter Benenson when he read about the imprisoned Portuguese students in 1960. Amnesty's members, staff, supporters, and volunteers are ordinary individuals outraged and roused to action by the fact that hundreds, perhaps thousands, of miles away, other people just like themselves are suffering barbaric treatment. The letter writers, lobbyists, and demonstrators who make up Amnesty are linked to the prisoners they are trying to help by one special quality — their common humanity.

In recent years, Peter Benenson has continued his work for Amnesty, although in a more limited capacity than in the early days. Although he no longer runs the worldwide organization, he still speaks for the movement and answers the hundreds of letters he receives from Amnesty members everywhere. Benenson has also helped to launch new campaigns, not necessarily associated with Amnesty, whenever he has seen a need. One project, naturally, was to found a society for people suffering from celiac disease and to educate the medical profession to be more aware of the complaint. Now most celiac patients in Britain are members, and there are similar societies in many parts of the world.

A more recent enterprise for Benenson was inspired by the 1989 revolutions that toppled tyranny in Eastern Europe. In an effort to strengthen Amnesty's organizational commitment to the abolition of torture, Benenson campaigned to have former torturers tried and brought to justice for their crimes against humanity.

Another concern is that Amnesty's work should not end with a prisoner's release. Many men, women, and children have emerged from prisons and torture chambers physically and emotionally shattered by their ordeal. They need tremendous support on many levels to begin living again as productive citizens.

Most of all, Benenson hopes Amnesty International will never lose its heart by becoming something other than a purely humanitarian organization, inspired by

Opposite: A letter-writing meeting for an Amnesty group in Holland. Over the years, the names of regimes that abuse human rights may have changed, but Amnesty's approach still remains fundamentally the same.

Below: A meeting of Amnesty's Japanese section. Since its creation in 1961, Amnesty has grown into the biggest human rights movement in the world.

55

Within the image, the protest signs read:

Where are they?

Where are they?

Where are they?

Where are they?

Where are they?

4 MONTHS PREGNANT:

WHERE IS THE CHILD?

Amnesty draws attention to the plight of men and women who disappeared in Chile after the 1973 military coup there. The graves of some missing Chileans were discovered in 1990 after the return of democracy.

the passionate moral indignation against oppression and injustice.

Whatever Amnesty has managed to achieve, its members and staff, including Peter Benenson himself, are always driven by the need to do more. There are prisoners throughout the world who need immediate attention, and each one is as important and urgent as any other. As one historian of the movement, Jonathan Power, puts it: "For every carnival, there are a hundred nights in the desert; for every release, another batch of prisoners; for every family reunited, another torn asunder; for every shout of exultation, a cry of suffering, as the heavy door shuts out the daylight for one more prisoner, leaving him to nurse his own wounds and

56

wait, when the morning arrives, for the tread of the official torturer or the executioner."

Victory over despair

Amnesty's interventions and its moral stand have made an enormous social and political impact all over the world. In 1974, a young Indian woman, Archana Guha, was arrested, beaten, and left paralyzed by a series of horrific tortures carried out by police in Calcutta. The government merely suspected that some of her relatives might be members of an extremist communist movement. She was held in detention without trial for over three years before being released in 1976.

Dressed in prison clothes, Amnesty members take part in an antitorture protest in 1985. Young people worldwide have been able to help thousands of prisoners and torture victims by drawing public attention to these abuses.

Journalist Viola Hernandez was held in detention in El Salvador for two-and-a-half years. Without letters from Amnesty groups around the world, she said, "our conditions would have been disastrous." Here Viola celebrates freedom with her five-year-old son, Alfonso.

In 1979, an Amnesty mission visiting India heard of her story and published details about it. Archana was still paralyzed from the waist down when Amnesty's Danish Medical Group took up her case in January 1980. They flew her from India to Denmark for intensive treatment for the injuries to her spine. After two months of therapy, she could get out of bed by herself and walk short distances without help.

Later, when she was back home in India, she joyfully wrote to thank the group. Her words can stand for the countless thousands of people all over the world for whom Amnesty International has meant a victory over hopelessness and despair: "My friends and relatives are simply astonished," she said. "Now I can walk and move! The secretary and colleagues of my school are waiting eagerly for the day when I'll be able to join them. I have improved much in walking and climbing the staircase. You have caused rebirth to me! You have given me new life!"

At the twentieth anniversary ceremony of Amnesty International in London, Peter Benenson offered a new slogan for the organization that has helped to free so many people held without just cause throughout the world — "Against Oblivion": "I have lit this candle today, in the words of Shakespeare, 'against oblivion' — so that the forgotten prisoners should always be remembered. We work in Amnesty *against oblivion*."

Haitian teacher Marc Romulus is reunited with his son Patrice after three years in prison. When a West German Amnesty group first took his case, the Haitian government claimed Marc "did not exist," and then said he was an "unrepentant terrorist." He was released in 1977.

The Universal Declaration of Human Rights

The Universal Declaration of Human Rights was adopted by the United Nations General Assembly in Paris in 1948. The thirty-article document contains definitions of everyone's civil, political, economic, social, and cultural rights. The preamble, or introduction, to this important declaration is as follows:

Preamble

Whereas recognition of the inherent dignity and of the equal and inalienable rights of all members of the human family is the foundation of freedom, justice and peace in the world,

Whereas disregard and contempt for human rights have resulted in barbarous acts which have outraged the conscience of mankind, and the advent of a world in which human beings shall enjoy freedom of speech and belief and freedom from fear and want has been proclaimed as the highest aspiration of the common people,

Whereas it is essential, if man is not to be compelled to have recourse, as a last resort, to rebellion against tyranny and oppression, that human rights should be protected by the rule of law,

Whereas it is essential to promote the development of friendly relations between nations,

Whereas the peoples of the United Nations have in the Charter reaffirmed their faith in fundamental human rights, in the dignity and worth of the human person and in the equal rights of men and women and have determined to promote social progress and better standards of life in larger freedom,

Whereas Member States have pledged themselves to achieve, in co-operation with the United Nations, the promotion of universal respect for and observance of human rights and fundamental freedoms,

Whereas a common understanding of these rights and freedoms is of the greatest importance for the full realization of this pledge,

Now, therefore,

The General Assembly

Proclaims this Universal Declaration of Human Rights as a common standard of achievement for all peoples and all nations, to the end that every individual and every organ of society, keeping this Declaration constantly in mind, shall strive by teaching and education to promote respect for these rights and freedoms and by progressive measures, national and international, to secure their universal and effective recognition and observance, both among the peoples of Member States themselves and among the peoples of territories under their jurisdiction.

For More Information . . .

Organizations

If you would like to find out more about human rights abuses around the world, the following organizations can provide you with more information. When you write to them, be sure to include your full name, age, and address, and be as specific as possible in your questions.

Amnesty International
(in the United States)
322 Eighth Avenue
New York, NY 10001
(in Canada)
130 Slater Street, Suite 900
Ottawa, Ontario K1P 6E2
Canada

Center of Concern
3700 Thirteenth Street NE
Washington, DC 20017

Human Rights Watch
485 Fifth Avenue
New York, NY 10017

International League for Human Rights
432 Park Avenue South, Room 1103
New York, NY 10016

Amnistie Internationale
3516 ave du Parc
Montreal, Quebec H2X 2H7
Canada

If you would like to get involved, the Children's Urgent Action Network can tell you about things you can do to help prisoners of conscience around the world, some of whom are people your own age. To find out more, write to

Children's Urgent Action Network
P.O. Box 1270
Nederland, CO 80466

Books

Anne Frank: The Diary of a Young Girl. Anne Frank (Doubleday)
Every Kid's Guide to Understanding Human Rights. Joy Berry (Childrens Press)
For the Love of Letter Writing. Wanda Lincoln and Murray Suid (Monday Morning Books)
How Many Days to America? A Thanksgiving Story. Eve Bunting (Clarion Books)
Human Rights. John Bradley (Franklin Watts)
Human Rights: Today's World. Charles Freeman (David & Charles)
Prison Life in America. Anna Kosof (Franklin Watts)
Taking A Stand Against Human Rights Abuse. Michael Kronenwetter (Franklin Watts)

Glossary

activism
    The process of either supporting or opposing a controversial issue through some means of positive action. Amnesty International is an activist organization that insists on basic human rights.

amnesty
A general pardon for people accused of crimes and offenses, thereby freeing them from punishment.

anti-Semitism
A particular type of prejudice whose holders persecute and are hostile to Jews solely because they are Jewish.

apartheid
A word that literally means "apart-hood." Under an apartheid system, races are kept separate by law. South Africa has operated under a system of apartheid since 1948.

bloc
A group of people, parties, or nations united by a common interest or purpose.

capitalism
An economic system in which wealth, property, business, and manufacturing are owned by individuals. In some capitalist countries, however, the government owns certain industries, such as those dealing with health care and transportation.

communism
A social system where the government controls all economic and political activities, and where, in theory, wealth is evenly distributed. There is no private ownership of property in a purely communist system.

coup
Short for *coup d'état*. A sudden, often violent, overthrow of a government.

democracy
A form of government based on protecting the rights of the people. A democracy is governed by the people, usually through elected representatives who act according to the desires of those who voted for them.

dictator
An absolute ruler who is not answerable to any authority but his or her own. Dictators are not usually elected by democratic processes; rather, they assume power by using military force or political guile.

diplomat
A person whose job involves handling or negotiating important issues and problems that may exist between his or her own country and some other country.

fascism
A form of government in which a single ruler controls the nation and makes decisions without regard for the will of the people. Fascist governments are aggressive toward other countries and oppressive toward their own people. Fascist governments tend to be military dictatorships.

Gulag
A Russian word that stands for the Chief Administration of Corrective Labor Camps. The Gulag was a system of prisons for dissidents and other opponents of the Soviet government. Here they were forced to work long hours under poor conditions. Many prisoners died from disease and starvation.

human rights

The basic rights to which every human being is entitled, without regard to race, religion, nationality, sex, age, or political beliefs. Human rights include equal access to food, clothing, shelter, and education. Privacy, freedom from torture and murder, freedom of speech and religious belief, the right to equal treatment under the law, and the right to vote are also human rights.

iron curtain

The name given by Winston Churchill to the border between Soviet-dominated Eastern Europe and the democracies of the West. Originally an imaginary barrier, in the 1950s it became a real one, when East Germany erected barbed-wire fences to prevent people from crossing the border into West Germany.

left-wing

A term describing liberal, progressive, or radical political beliefs. Left-wing political thinkers and activists tend to value political change in the name of the greater well-being of the common people.

Nobel Prizes

Yearly awards given for work in certain areas. Nobel Prizes are awarded in chemistry, physics, economics, medicine or physiology, and literature, and for promoting peace. Amnesty International won the Nobel Peace Prize in 1977.

prisoner of conscience

Anyone who is held in prison or persecuted for his or her beliefs, religion, language, race, sex, or ethnic origin. Prisoners of conscience can be from any walk of life — writers, musicians, artists, teachers, politicians, or anyone else.

refugee

A person who flees from one place to another to escape danger or persecution.

right-wing

A term describing conservative or reactionary political beliefs. Right-wing political thinkers and activists value social conformity and adherence to traditional values and roles, and generally favor a free-market economy and uncontrolled property rights.

socialism

A system of government under which control and ownership of production and distribution of at least certain goods and services is in the hands of the community as a whole.

tyranny

The unjust and cruel use of power.

Chronology

1921   **July 31** — Peter Benenson is born in London, England, to Harold Solomon and Flora Benenson Solomon.

1930   Harold Solomon dies. Peter later takes his mother's birth name, Benenson, as his own in honor of his Russian maternal grandfather, Grigori Benenson.

1936	The Spanish Civil War begins. It lasts until 1939.
1937	Peter, aged sixteen, helps organize school support for the Spanish Relief Committee and "adopts" a baby.
1938	Peter works to help Jews escape from Adolf Hitler's Germany. He and schoolmates raise enough money for two young German Jews to be educated in Great Britain.
1939	**September 1** — World War II begins. Shortly after the war starts, Peter volunteers for the Royal Navy but is turned down. He becomes a student at Oxford University.
1940	Benenson begins his military service.
1945	World War II ends. Benenson studies law while waiting to be dismissed from military service.
1947	Benenson leaves the army and starts a career as a lawyer. He joins Britain's Labour party and acts as an observer for the Trade Union Congress (TUC) at a trial in Spain.
1948	**December 10** — The United Nations General Assembly adopts the Universal Declaration of Human Rights.
1956	Benenson forms "Justice," a tripartisan group of British lawyers that helps people persecuted by their own countries' legal systems. Justice later becomes the British section of the International Commission of Jurists.
1959	Benenson, suffering from tropical sprue, goes to Italy on his doctor's orders for six months to recuperate. While he is there, he decides to give up his legal career.
1960	**October** — Benenson returns to the United Kingdom from his trip abroad. **November** — Benenson is outraged when he reads an article in London's *Daily Telegraph* about two students who have been imprisoned in Portugal for raising their glasses in a toast to liberty. The idea for Amnesty is conceived.
1961	**May 28** — Peter Benenson launches an "Appeal for Amnesty, 1961." His article "The Forgotten Prisoners," Amnesty International's manifesto, appears simultaneously in key newspapers around the world. His book, *Persecution 1961*, setting out the extent of the crisis, is published as the campaign opens. Amnesty undertakes its first mission on behalf of a prisoner of conscience — to Czechoslovakia to appeal for the release of Archbishop Josef Beran. The first Amnesty group overseas is founded in West Germany. Holland, Switzerland, Italy, and France follow before the end of the year.
1962	Amnesty groups are founded in Norway, Sweden, and Denmark. At a conference in Belgium, all the national groups decide to set up a permanent organization that will be known as Amnesty International. Irish statesman Sean MacBride is chosen as the group's chairperson.
1964	Benenson goes to Haiti to perform an undercover research mission for

Amnesty International. After his report is published in the French newspaper *Le Monde*, Haiti expels British, French, and United States diplomats.

1967   **March** — Benenson gives up his day-to-day involvement with Amnesty International. Eric Baker is selected to run the organization. There are now 410 Amnesty groups in eighteen countries.
A ten-year period begins in the United States during which there are no executions. During this time, increasing numbers of Americans call for permanently banning the death penalty.

1972   Amnesty International launches a worldwide campaign for the abolition of the use of torture.
The U.S. Supreme Court rules that prevailing state laws on capital punishment are unconstitutional.

1974   Sean MacBride, Amnesty International's chairperson, wins the Nobel Peace Prize for his efforts on behalf of human rights.

1976   The U.S. Supreme Court reverses its decision on the death penalty. Over the next decade, more than eighty people are executed in the United States.

1977   Amnesty International is awarded the Nobel Peace Prize.
December — In Stockholm, Amnesty International holds a conference on the abolition of the death penalty.

1978   Amnesty International is awarded the United Nations Human Rights Prize.

1981   **April** — In London, Amnesty International holds a candle-lighting ceremony to mark its twentieth anniversary.

1983   Amnesty International publishes a special report on political killings by governments.

1984   Amnesty International renews its campaign for the abolition of torture. It draws up a twelve-point prevention plan.

1985   Amnesty International issues a paper on the imprisonment of conscientious objectors to compulsory military service. It provides the details of cases from fourteen countries.

1990   With 700,000 members in 150 countries, Amnesty International is the largest human rights organization in the world.

Index